PBY Catalina

Written by David Doyle

In Action®

Color Art by Don Greer

Line Illustrations by Todd Sturgell

Squadron Signal®
Publications

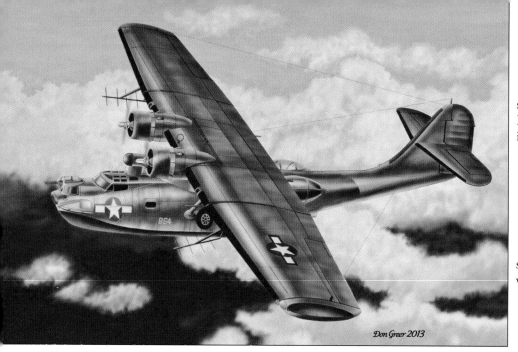

(Front Cover) In the Pacific, some of the lumbering Catalina patrol bombers donned an overall black camouflage scheme and served as night raiders. Flying from Guadalcanal in 1944, this "Black Cat" PBY-5A assigned to Patrol Squadron 54 features a black paint scheme, a radome on the turtle deck aft of the cockpit canopy, and an "eyeball" turret.

(Back Cover) The Catalina entered service at a time when Naval aircraft wore colorful paint schemes. In 1937, this PBY-1 11-P-9 of Patrol Squadron 11F dazzled in a paint scheme of overall Aluminum, with Chrome Yellow wing tops and black anti-fouling paint on the hull up to the waterline.

About the In Action® Series

In Action® books, despite the title of the genre, are books that trace the development of a single type of aircraft, armored vehicle, or ship from prototype to the final production variant. Experimental or "one-off" variants can also be included. Our first In Action® book was printed in 1971.

Hardcover ISBN 978-0-89747-739-0
Softcover ISBN 978-0-89747-740-6

 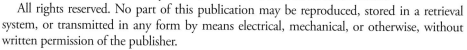

Proudly printed in the U.S.A.
Copyright 2013 Squadron/Signal Publications
1115 Crowley Drive, Carrollton, TX 75006-1312 U.S.A.

Military/Combat Photographs and Snapshots

If you have any photos of aircraft, armor, soldiers, or ships of any nation, particularly wartime snapshots, why not share them with us and help make Squadron/Signal's books all the more interesting and complete in the future? Any photograph sent to us will be copied and returned. Electronic images are preferred. The donor will be fully credited for any photos used. Please send them to:

Squadron/Signal Publications
1115 Crowley Drive
Carrollton, TX 75006-1312 U.S.A.
www.SquadronSignalPublications.com

(Title Page) Although ungainly, slow, and developed for the unglamorous role of maritime patrol, the PBY Catalina was a durable, dependable, and versatile flying boat. This PBY-5A was photographed off the Aleutian Islands. (Stan Piet Collection)

Acknowledgments

This book would not have been possible without the generous assistance and resources of many friends and institutions. Among them, Tom Kailbourn; Tracy White; Stan Piet; Scott Taylor; Dana Bell; the National Museum of Naval Aviation; the National Museum of the United States Air Force; the San Diego Air and Space Museum; the American Aviation Historical Society; the Naval History and Heritage Command and the National Archives. Through the hard work of my friends at Squadron Signal Publications, our research and writing efforts were converted to the volume presented here. Many of the photos in this book were scanned by my wife Denise, without whose help and support this book would not have been possible.

Introduction

The Consolidated PBY is the most readily recognized – and widely produced – flying boat design ever made. The aircraft, which came to be known as the Catalina, has it origins in Consolidated's 1932 Model 28. The Model 28 went from drawing board into the air as the XP3Y-1, first flown on 21 March 1935. The new aircraft was the first flying boat designed to be armed with bombs and torpedoes and, accordingly, the Navy redesignated the aircraft XPBY-1.

After test flights of the new aircraft, and two redesigns of the rudder, a production order was placed for 60 aircraft, which were to be assembled at Consolidated's new facility in San Diego, California. These were followed in short order by 50 PBY-2 aircraft.

This order was followed by 66 PBY-3 and 33 PBY-4 aircraft. Thirty of a new model, the 28-5 (PBY-5), were first ordered by the French. After France capitulated to Germany in 1940, these aircraft were instead delivered to Great Britain, where they were bestowed the name "Catalina." Pleased with the aircraft (Britain had evaluated a PBY-4 earlier), the Commonwealth placed additional orders.

In December 1939 the U.S. Navy ordered 200 PBY-5s, the first really large order for the aircraft placed by the American military. Up to this point, all the Catalinas had been true flying boats, requiring beaching gear to come ashore. Now, however, it was considered advantageous for the airplane to be an amphibian. Accordingly, the last production PBY-4, Bureau Number (BuNo.) 1245, was outfitted with retractable landing gear, becoming the XPBY-5A. It was first flown in this configuration on 22 November 1939.

In February 1928, the U.S. Navy granted Consolidated Aircraft a contract to produce a prototype of the Navy's first monoplane flying boat. It featured two vertical tails, an open cockpit, and two Pratt & Whitney engines. The XPY-1 first took to the air on 10 January 1929. (San Diego Air and Space Museum)

The next step in Consolidated Aircraft's development of flying boats, the XP2Y-1 prototype, was an improvement of the XPY-1. Contracted for on 26 May 1931, the aircraft was initially powered by a trio of 575-horsepower Wright Cyclone engines, and featured a short wing beneath the main airfoil. (San Diego Air and Space Museum)

Shortly after the XP2Y-1's first flight on 26 March 1932 and the start of its test program, it was determined that the top-mounted engine offered no real benefit, and was eliminated. In addition to the second wing, the XP2Y-1 also differed from the XPY-1 by having an enclosed cockpit.

The Navy was so pleased with the results of this version that a contract modification specified that the last 33 PBY-5 aircraft on order were to be completed as PBY-5A aircraft instead. Deliveries of these planes began in October 1941. Beyond these 33 aircraft, in November 1940 the Navy had ordered a further 134 PBY-5As. Following the Japanese attack on Pearl Harbor, 635 more PBY-5A aircraft were ordered from Consolidated by the Navy. However, some of these were delivered to Australia, Britain, Canada, and the Free French, in addition to the U.S. Army. In Army service, they were designated OA-10.

Boeing of Canada also began producing this aircraft during 1940, and it was joined by Canadian Vickers. Two-hundred thirty of the latter were delivered to the U.S. Army Air Force, where they were referred to as OA-10A.

As production of the PBY-5A progressed, various changes were introduced, including the installation of a search radar above the cockpit, and an improved bow machine gun turret.

The PBY-5A was superceded by the PBY-6A, which had an improved tail design. Orders were placed for 900 of these aircraft to be built at Consolidated's New Orleans plant, but when Germany surrendered in May 1945, the order was canceled. Only 175 of the PBY-6As had been completed. Seventy-five of those went to the U.S. Army under the designation OA-10B, and 48 were supplied to the Soviet Union. The PBY-6A was the last of the Catalinas built by Consolidated, whose total production of the type was 2,398 aircraft. A further 900 were built by Boeing of Canada, Canadian Vickers, and the Naval Aircraft Factory.

In July 1931, the Navy granted Consolidated a contract for 23 P2Y-1s. The last of those aircraft was converted to the XP2Y-2, with engines enclosed in nacelles faired into the leading edge of the upper wing, rather than underslung as on the P2Y-1.

The new engine installation and a few other improvements brought about a 10-mile-per-hour increase in the aircraft's top speed and an increase in range. Suitably impressed, the Navy ordered 23 of the new model, which was designated the P2Y-3. (San Diego Air and Space Museum)

So pleased was the Navy with the improved performance of the P2Y-3 that a conversion program was undertaken on the P2Y-1. Dubbed the Ranger, all the P2Y-1 aircraft received the new engine installation and were redesignated P2Y-2. (San Diego Air and Space Museum)

The XP3Y-1 grew out of a 1932 U.S. Navy requirement for a new patrol flying boat with a gross weight of 25,000 pounds and a range of 3,000 miles at a 100 mile per hour cruising speed. The following year, the Navy issued Consolidated a contract to produce one prototype aircraft based on the company's design. The result was the XP3Y-1, which made its first flight on 28 March 1935. As can be seen in this photo of the plane during tests at Naval Air Station (NAS) Anacostia on 23 April 1935, the plane had the hallmarks of what would become the PBY Catalina, including the parasol wing mounted on a pylon, retractable floats, low cockpit canopy, and provisions for a bow turret. (American Aviation Historical Society)

Two handlers dressed in wetsuits stand in the water next to the XP3Y-1 at Anacostia while another handler leans over the port strut. Consolidated Aircraft designated the XP3Y-1 as Model 28, while the U.S. Navy assigned it Bureau Number (BuNo) 9459. (National Museum of Naval Aviation)

The XP3Y-1 was photographed on 10 April 1935, several weeks after its initial flight. The floats were mounted on retracting struts; when raised, the floats formed the actual wingtips. Unlike the XPY-1 and P2Y, the XP3Y-1 had a single vertical fin and rudder. (San Diego Air and Space Museum)

The XP3Y-1's rudder underwent several revisions. Here is the first design, with a trailing edge that was straight and vertical. As was the case with the P2Ys, the engines of the XP3Y-1 were mounted in nacelles protruding from the leading edge of the wing. (San Diego Air and Space Museum)

The XP3Y-1 rests on the water at NAS Anacostia, District of Columbia, on 23 April 1935 during trials. During trials several months later, problems were encountered with the directional stability of the rudder, and Consolidated took measures to correct them. (San Diego Air and Space Museum)

Consolidated's fix for the XP3Y-1's rudder problems was to install a redesigned rudder on the tail. It had a straight trailing edge like that of the first rudder, but the trailing edge was set at an angle, as seen in this photo of the plane lying in the water near an *Omaha*-class light cruiser. (San Diego Air and Space Museum)

Crewmen manhandle the XP3Y-1 while Naval officers observe the proceedings. The second design of the rudder is present. Aft of the wing on each side of the hull was a sliding panel with a small window, and a man is standing up in the open hatch. (San Diego Air and Space Museum)

Commanded by K. McGinnis, the crew of the XP3Y-1 pose for a photo at the time the aircraft set a new nonstop flight record of 3,443 miles, from Panama to NAS Alameda in October 1935. The floats are retracted, showing how they form the wingtips when raised. (National Museum of Naval Aviation)

The XP3Y-1 takes off during mid-1936. After the second version of the rudder exhibited problems, a third version, seen here, was installed. This rudder's trailing edge had a curved shape. Black bituminous asphalt paint is on the bottom of the hull and floats. (San Diego Air and Space Museum)

During Consolidated's final tests of the plane, the XP3Y-1 flies over San Diego Bay on 16 May 1936, with North Island at the center of the photo and the harbor at the bottom. Less than a week later, the company would transfer the aircraft to the Navy. (National Museum of Naval Aviation)

The XP3Y-1 displays its port side during a flight over the hills near San Diego, California, on 16 May 1936. Once this prototype had demonstrated the capability of carrying bombs, it was redesignated XPBY-1, the "B" standing for bomber. (San Diego Air and Space Museum)

In 1937, this PBY-1 of VP-11 had a paint scheme of Aluminum above the waterline, Black below the waterline, and Chrome Yellow wing top. Control surfaces were doped fabric. The "11-P-9" code on the side of the hull referred to the ninth aircraft of VP-11.

Following successful initial tests of the XP3Y-1/XPBY-1 prototype in the spring of 1935, the U.S. Navy contracted with Consolidated Aircraft in June 1935 for 60 PBY-1s. Virtually identical to the prototype, the PBY-1 was delivered to the Navy, beginning in September 1936. Powering this flying boat were two Pratt & Whitney R-1830-64 engines. Shown here is a PBY-1 of Utility Squadron 4 (VJ-4), marked with the so-called Neutrality Patrol national insignia between the cockpit and the bow turret, as specified in a 19 March 1940 directive by the Bureau of Aeronautics. Visible atop the hull (as the fuselage was called) aft of the wing is a tow-target reel. (American Aviation Historical Society)

The first PBY-1, BuNo 0102, sits on a ramp on 22 October 1936. It bears markings for VP-6 and is fitted with beaching gear, consisting of detachable landing gear attached to the sides of the hull below the wing and on the underside of the rear of the hull. (National Museum of Naval Aviation)

Seen from the front on 22 October 1936, PBY-1 number one, assigned to VP-6, demonstrates just how little clearance there was between the two propellers. Also evident is the extent to which the bow turret diminished the pilot's and copilot's field of view forward. (National Archives)

As evident in this view of the PBY-1 from the starboard side, the X-shaped brace for the float assembly is actually composed of two V-shaped braces joined together. These braces also serve as the retraction link for the float. (National Archives)

In a view from the aft starboard quarter of the first PBY-1, further details of the arrangement of the floats and their braces are visible. Faintly visible at the top center of the wing is the numeral 6, representing VP-6, redesignated VP-23 in 1939. (National Archives)

A view of the first PBY-1 from directly aft emphasizes the squat shape of the hull and the positioning of the horizontal stabilizers. In addition to the pylon, which was the main support for the wing, there were two diagonal braces on each side. (National Archives)

The inboard end of the port elevator of the first PBY-1 is displayed; it was angled to give clearance to the movement of the rudder. The elevators would be redesigned for the PBY-2. Also in view is the tail beaching gear and the Bureau Number on the vertical fin. (National Archives)

A closer view is offered of the tail beaching gear on a PBY-1. Two 5.00 x 4 aluminum-alloy wheels with 5.00 x 4 six-ply, smooth-contour rubber tires are on a shock-mounted swiveling knuckle at the bottom of a V-strut. This V-strut is secured to attachment points on the bottom of the hull. The V-strut is strengthened with a single strut attached to the swiveling knuckle and secured with a pin to the towing lug at the upper right of the photo. Attached to the swivel knuckle is a socket into which is inserted the steering bar. (National Archives)

The PBY-1 had an anchor, stowed in the small compartment with the door open. One end of the anchor line is secured to the anchor, and the other end leads to the anchor cable reel inside the anchor box. A line called the pendant, which was used to take up the weight of the anchor, is secured on one end to the anchor cable and on the other end to the fitting visible on the bottom of the hull. Another line, called the lizard, is secured on one end to the pendant and on the other to the mooring post by the turret. (National Archives)

The port main beaching gear of a PBY-1 is displayed close-up in a 3 October 1936 Consolidated factory photo. It consisted of a rigid strut with two 11.00 x 12 Hayes wheels with 11.00 x 12 eight-ply, smooth-contour Goodrich low-pressure tires on a swiveling knuckle. The top of the strut was secured to the upper fitting, recessed in the bottom of the fairing of the forward wing strut. Two brackets on the strut held two long pins, which secured the bottom bracket to the lower fitting, riveted to the chine of the hull. (National Archives)

A Consolidated Aircraft factory photo dated 15 July 1936 illustrates the aluminum-alloy plating on the forward part of the hull of a partially completed PBY-1. A good view is available of the turret ring, bombardier's window, and anchor box hatch. (National Archives)

An October 1936 Consolidated Aircraft photo shows the bow turret, armed with a Browning .30-caliber machine gun. Although the turret had Plexiglas windows, there was a large open area on the roof of the turret. Also shown is the door of the anchor box. (National Archives)

The anchor is folded up for storage in its compartment on the port side of the bow. Placards with instructions on handling the anchor and its lines are affixed to the inside of the door. The manila rope visible inside the compartment is the lizard. At the top of the door is a snap fitting for holding the door open. Just aft of the anchor box is a retractable step. To the right is an on/off switch for the anchor lights. To the upper left, a part of one of the clear panels of the bow turret is in view. (National Archives)

In a 1936 view inside the bombardier's compartment in the bow of a PBY-1, the .30-caliber machine gun for the turret is stowed in brackets on the starboard side of the compartment. The bombardier doubled as turret gunner in the PBYs. To the left are: bombardier's seat, kneeling cushion, bombardier's window and, at the upper left, the turret. The round panel to the right of the bombardier's window was removable and allowed the bombardier to clean the bomb-aiming window in flight if necessary. (National Archives)

The port wingtip float is shown in the extended position in a Consolidated Aircraft photo from October 1936. These floats were of all-metal construction, with aluminum-alloy stressed skin, and they gave the PBY-1 lateral stability while on the water. A recess on the underside of the wing accommodated the drag panel (the major support structure for the float) and the V-struts when the float was raised. A slot in that recess provided room for movement of the screw jack, which actuated the raising and lowering of the float. (National Archives)

The port float is raised, showing how the float formed the wingtip. Also apparent is the manner in which the drag panel of the float assembly fits in the recess in the wing. Next to the float on the leading edge of the wing is the red-colored port navigation light. (National Archives)

Because of the height of the engines of the Catalina, Consolidated Aircraft developed an A-frame boom that attached to the engine and was braced by stays and fitted with a hoist, to lift or lower the propeller when it was necessary to perform maintenance. (National Archives)

The starboard engine installation of a PBY-1 is viewed from the wing facing forward. In the foreground, with the black box on top, is the top of the starboard oil tank, with a capacity of 47 U.S. gallons. Jutting up from the tank is the oil filler tube and cap. On either side of the oil filler tube is an engine exhaust outlet. In the background, some of the hinged panels of the engine cowl are open. (National Archives)

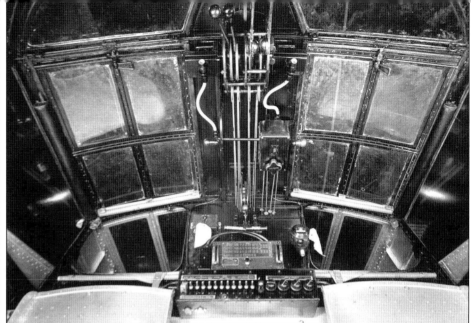

The cockpit of a PBY-1 is viewed from bulkhead number two at the rear of the compartment, facing forward. The pilot's seat is to the left and the copilot's seat is to the right. The control wheels are on a control yoke that extends across the cockpit. (National Archives)

From the center of the cockpit facing upward and aft, between the seats on bulkhead two are the pilot's communications controls and electrical panel. On the roof are windows that double as escape hatch doors, and the pilot's throttle and fuel mixture controls. (National Archives)

This view of the bombardier's compartment of a PBY-1 was taken from the cockpit through an open door in a canvas screen meant to keep drafts out of the cockpit. To the right are racks for .30-caliber ammunition boxes; stowed to the left is the turret cover. (National Archives)

Tests of the XP3Y-1 had proven that flying boat's aptitude as a bomber, and provisions for mounting bombs were designed into the PBY-1. Six 100-pound bombs are shackled to two bomb racks under the wing of a PBY-1 in a 24 September 1936 photo. (National Archives)

Larger bombs could also be carried on the PBY-1, such as this inert 500-pound bomb being hoisted to a bomb rack with a streamlined fairing. On the near side of the bomb is a portable work platform, secured to fasteners on the bottom of the wing. (National Archives)

A torpedo could also be carried under each wing, as indicated in this September 1937 photo of a Mk. 13 torpedo secured to a rack under the wing of a PBY-1. More details are visible of the portable platforms, which greatly facilitated the work of the crews. (National Archives)

A 1,000-pound bomb is being hoisted to the rack under the port side of the wing of a PBY-1. PBYs could carry the Mk. 5, Mk. 9, or Mk. 13 1,000-pound bomb, each with the Mk. 21 nose fuse and Mk. 23 tail fuse. In addition, PBYs could carry the Mk. 7 water-filled practice bomb. A protective cover of what appears to be kraft paper has been applied to the upper part of the hull of the flying boat. Some of the support frame for the engine is at the upper left. (National Archives)

The radio/navigation compartment of a PBY-1, directly aft of the cockpit, is viewed facing forward. To the left are the navigator's table and seat. On the right side of the compartment are the radioman's seat and radio transmitting equipment. (National Archives)

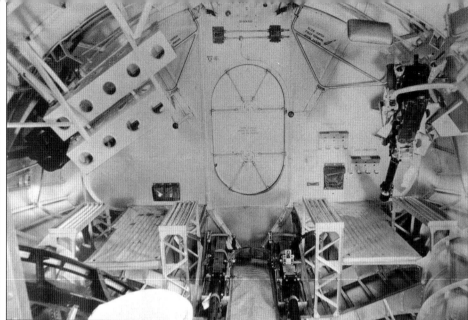

The waist compartment of a PBY-1 is viewed facing forward, with bulkhead number six, a watertight bulkhead, in the background. A machine gun is stowed on each side of the hull, and two extra machine guns are secured on each side of the catwalk. (National Archives)

The port waist hatch (top) and the .30-caliber machine gun and mount for that position are viewed. The gun is mounted a swiveling stirrup, allowing the gun to be swung down and stored or rapidly restored to firing position. To the left are ammunition-box racks. (National Archives)

The position of the starboard waist hatch door when opened is shown, along with a .50-caliber machine gun in its firing position. Small stencils indicate where a ladder was to be hooked over the bottom of the hatch. A retractable post is aft of the hatch. (National Archives)

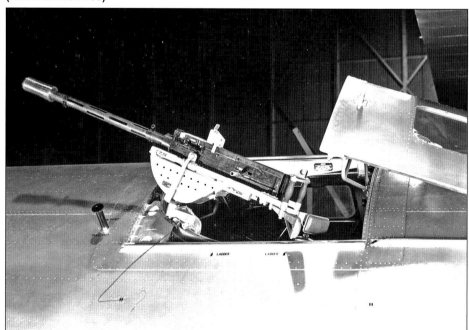

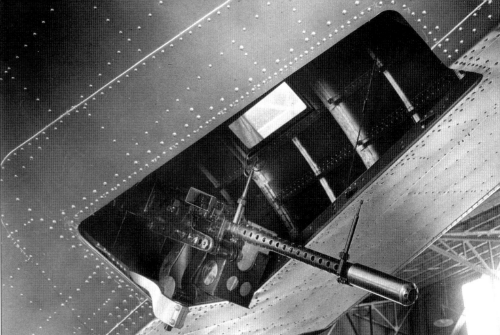

Aft of the waist compartment in the PBY-1 was a tunnel-gun position, with a .30-caliber machine gun on a swiveling mount called the stirrup (shown here in the stowed position). The gun could be fired through the hatch on the bottom of the hull to the far left. (National Archives)

A .30-caliber machine gun with ring and bead sights is pointing out of the hatch in the tunnel position; the aft part of the hull is to the upper right. When the hatch door was open, it was stowed in a vertical position next to the hatch inside the aircraft. (National Archives)

The number-eleven aircraft of Patrol Squadron 12 (VP-12) in 1937 was this PBY-1. The two horizontal stripes on the rudder denoted Patrol Wing 1 (PatWing 1). National insignia at this stage of the PBY's development were limited to the wings.

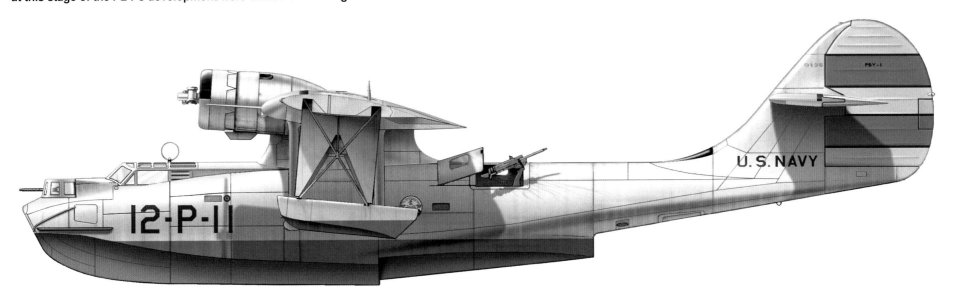

PBYs of Patrol Squadron 12, to the left, and Patrol Squadron 9, on the right, are assembled on the ramp at San Diego in June 1938, prior to taking off on a loose-formation flight to Seattle. Fabric covers are over the cowls and cockpit canopies. (National Museum of Naval Aviation)

PBY-1 BuNo 0135 of VP-12F (redesignated VP-12 on 1 October 1937) is anchored in Lake Washington near Seattle, in 1937. The number 11 in its markings indicated that it was the second aircraft in the fourth section; there were three aircraft in each section. (National Museum of Naval Aviation)

PBY-1 BuNo 0156 participates in fleet tactical exercises on 17 November 1937. The top of the wing was Chrome Yellow, with a black section in the middle of it. Metal surfaces on the hull were coated with Aluminum paint and fabric surfaces with Aluminum dope. (National Archives)

On 13 April 1937, PBY-1 BuNo 0124 of VP-11F approaches the coast of Oahu near Honolulu, the floats extended preparatory to landing. This was part of a 12-plane flight that had made the ocean crossing from San Diego under Lt. Col. L. A. Pope. (National Museum of Naval Aviation)

Consolidated Aircraft sold a number of PBYs commercially for civilian and government use. The first such sale was of this Model 28-1, the designation for an unarmed, all-weather PBY-1. The American Museum of Natural History acquired it in early 1937 for one of its research associates, Richard Archbold, to use on a scientific expedition to Dutch New Guinea. Archbold made several shakedown flights in the aircraft, nicknamed *Guba* after the Papuan word for "fierce storm," but before he was scheduled to leave for Dutch New Guinea, he sold the plane to the Soviets, who planned to employ it in a search for Sigizmund Levanevsky and his expeditionary team, who were lost during a flight over the North Pole on 13 August 1937. Despite an extensive international search effort, Levanevsky and his crew were never located. (National Museum of Naval Aviation)

On 25 July 1936, the U.S. Navy issued a contract for 50 PBY-2s to Consolidated Aircraft. Outwardly, the PBY-2 was virtually identical to the PBY-1 with the exception of a new feature in the empennage: instead of the PBY-1's elevators, which had angled inner edges to give clearance to the rudder, a new horizontal stabilizer was designed with a center section incorporating a complete chord. A cutout in the rudder permitted it to turn to port or starboard over the rear part of the horizontal stabilizer. Redesigned elevators had inboard edges set at right angles to the leading edges of the elevators, and also spaced outboard from the rudder. Seen here is the PBY-2, BuNo 0454, in VP-11F markings in May 1937. (National Archives)

PBY-2 BuNo 0454 rests on a tarmac at Consolidated Aircraft's San Diego plant on 15 May 1937. This model still retained the sliding hatch doors with small windows on top of the hull aft of the wing. A good view is offered of the lowered starboard float. (National Archives)

The engine nacelles and wing pylon of a PBY-2 are highlighted in a 22 May 1937 factory photo. At the bottoms of the nacelles are air intakes for the updraft carburetors. To the left is the starboard oil-cooler air intake. A RDF loop antenna is to the lower right. (National Archives)

A subassembly of a PBY-2 horizontal stabilizer, elevators, and the upper part of the vertical fin illustrates how the center part of the horizontal stabilizer formed a complete airfoil chord, with the inboard edges of the elevators shaped to fit within the stabilizer. (National Archives)

The empennage of the first PBY-2, BuNo 0454, is displayed. From this angle, it is noticeable how the rudder is cut out around the rear center part of the horizontal elevator. This is an important feature in differentiating the PBY-1 from the PBY-2 (and PBY-3). (National Archives)

The first PBY-2 is viewed from aft in a 15 May 1937 photograph. Even from this angle, the newly designed horizontal stabilizer and elevators are apparent. Until the advent of the clear bubbles in the waist of later PBYs, visibility to the rear was a problem. (National Archives)

The number-one PBY-2 is observed from the port aft quarter. The aft step of the hull, the breaker step, which terminates in a V shape forward of the aft beaching gear, is visible. The rear of the forward step, the taper step, is directly below the aft wing struts. (National Archives)

The forward and aft steps of PBY-2 BuNo 0454 are visible. Getting "up on the step" is an essential element of flying boat design, providing the pilot with a means of achieving minimal friction between the bottom of the hull and the water, ensuring a good takeoff. (National Archives)

At San Diego on 15 May 1937, a photographer captured this frontal view of the first PBY-2. Dominating the front end of the hull is the turret, which obscured the pilot's and copilot's view straight ahead and downward. The ground clearance of the hull is visible. (National Archives)

Engines running, a PBY-2 assigned to duty at NAS Jacksonville, Florida, is being prepared for towing on 5 June 1942. A crewman is securing a line from the tractor in the background to the tow ring on the underside of the hull adjacent to the aft beaching gear. (National Museum of Naval Aviation)

The same PBY-2 seen in the preceding photo is being eased down a ramp lined with beaching gears. The beaching gear is still attached to the hull, and the crewmen walking along the aircraft will remove the beaching gear when the aircraft is afloat. (National Museum of Naval Aviation)

While members of the flight crew watch something in the sky, PBY-2 BuNo 0490 rests in water along a shore, a portable ramp alongside it. This flying boat saw much service in Florida, where it experienced at least three accidents between 1940 and 1944. (National Museum of Naval Aviation)

The first U.S. Navy aircraft to be fitted with radar equipment was this PBY-2, BuNo 0456. The plane was at NAS Anacostia in October 1940, conducting tests of the system for the Naval Research Laboratory. Various arrays of antennas are visible on the hull. (American Aviation Historical Society)

After the American Museum of Natural History transferred *Guba* to the Soviet Union, in December 1937 the museum acquired a second flying boat, a PBY-2 nicknamed *Guba II*, for Dr. Richard Archbold's scientific expedition to New Guinea. (San Diego Air and Space Museum)

Guba II's markings were virtually identical of the original *Guba*. In addition to Archbold's personal insignia, two identifying characteristics of *Guba II* are visible: an RDF "football" antenna atop the wing, and the pitot tube and mast atop the canopy. (San Diego Air and Space Museum)

U.S. Navy Production

MODEL	Gross Weight	Max Speed @Altitude	Service Ceiling	Patrol Range	Number built	First Delivery	Serial Numbers
XPBY-1	20,226 lbs	184 MPH@8,000ft	24,000	2,070	1	May 1936	9459
PBY-1	22,336 lbs	175 MPH@8,000ft	20,900	2,115	60	Sept 1936	0102-0161
PBY-2	22,490 lbs	178 MPH@8,000ft	21,100	2131	50	May 1937	0454-0503
PBY-3	22,713 lbs	191 MPH@12,000ft	24,400	2175	66	Nov 1937	0842-0907
PBY-4	24,813 lbs	198 MPH@12,000ft	24,100	2070	32	May 1938	1213-1244
XPBY-5A	-	-	-	-	1	Nov 1939	1245
PBY-5	31,813 lbs	195 MPH@7,000ft	17,700	2860	684	Sept 1940	2289-2455, 04425-04514;08124-08549; 63992
PBY-5A	33,975 lbs	180 MPH@7,000ft	14,700	2545	802	Oct 1941	2456-2488; 7243-7302; 05972-05045; 02948-02977; 04399-04420; 08030-08123; 33960-34059; 46450-46579; 48252-48451; 46580-46638
PBY-6A	34,550 lbs	178 MPH @7,000ft	16,200	2535	175	May 1945	46639-46698; 46724; 63993-64106
PBN-1	36,553 lbs	186 MPH @6,700 ft	15,100	2590	155	Feb 1943	02791-02946

The first PBY-3, BuNo 0842, takes flight. This model varied from the PBY-2 primarily in the installation of Pratt & Whitney R-1830-66 engines, rated at 900 horsepower, an increase of 50 horsepower over the Pratt & Whitney R-1830-64 used in the PBY-1 and PBY-2. The one noticeable difference of the PBY-3 over the PBY-2 was the intake for the downdraft carburetors, which were on top of the engine nacelles. The U.S. Navy contracted for 66 PBY-3s on 27 November 1936; the first one was delivered in November 1937 and the last was delivered in August 1938. (National Museum of Naval Aviation)

Three PBY-3s of VP-41 fly over Cape St. Elias, Alaska Territory, around 1939, displaying the checkerboard tail markings of Patrol Wing (Patwing) 4. This squadron had been redesignated from VP-16 on 1 July 1939 and received its first PBY-3s in June 1938. (National Museum of Naval Aviation)

A PBY-3 taxis in water. The paint scheme appears to have been aluminum, with a yellow wing top with a black walkway area on the wing. Atop the center of the wing is the RDF loop antenna; many PBY-3s had this antenna positioned on top of the cockpit canopy. (Stan Piet Collection)

The port engine nacelle of a PBY-3 is viewed from atop the wing. The cowl panels and cowl flaps have been removed, exposing to view the inner framework of the cowl. Protruding above all is the carburetor air intake, flanked on each side by an engine exhaust port. The round object aft of the carburetor air intake is the access door for the port oil filler neck and cap. The dark panel at the bottom is a structural inspection door. (National Archives)

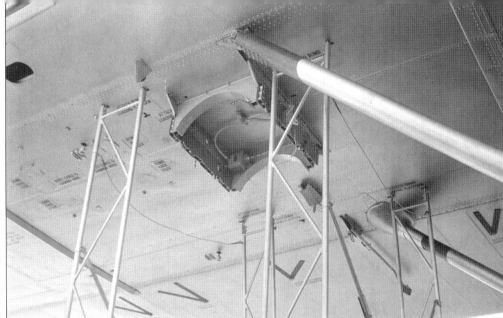

Occasionally, PBYs suffered mishaps during landings and takeoffs on water. This one, assigned to VP-5, suffered a nearly severed tail section, but the wing and its struts are still intact. A floating crane is in the process of salvaging the wreck off San Diego. (San Diego Air and Space Museum)

A Consolidated Aircraft factory photo from September 1937 shows a torpedo rack and related accessories installed under the starboard side of a PBY-3 wing. The stanchions of portable work platforms are inserted into T-shaped openings on the skin of the wing. (National Archives)

A torpedo director is on the dash above the instrument panel in the cockpit in a PBY-3. It included a simple computing mechanism and provided the pilot with the proper bearings for releasing the torpedo. The pilot or copilot controlled the release of the torpedoes. (National Archives)

Three PBY-3s assigned to NAS Corpus Christi fly over the Gulf of Mexico. They wear national insignia of the type in use from May 1942 to June 1943. The wingtops are a shade of yellow, and the hulls are evidently a shade of nonspecular blue or blue-gray. (Stan Piet Collection)

Crewman heave on a mooring line attached to the aft tow eye of a PBY-3 at NAS Corpus Christi. To install or remove the beaching gear, to moor the flying boat or secure tow lines to it, to steady the craft, and to perform other tasks, it was necessary for handlers to enter the water. When the water was warm, swimsuits were in order for PBY handlers; when it was cold, wetsuits were worn. The national insignia on this PBY-3 have red circles within the white stars. (Stan Piet Collection)

Crewmen at the seaplane ramp at NAS Corpus Christi rig a portable walkway next to a PBY-3, to enable the crew to enter or debark without getting themselves or their equipment wet. The man under the tail is securing a mooring line to the aft tow eye. (Stan Piet Collection)

A PBY-3 assigned to VN-4D8, a training squadron at NAS Pensacola, taxis on the water. The plane's number, 91, is in black on each side of the wing. The national insignia are of the type without the red circle in the center, in use from May 1942 to June 1943. (Stan Piet Collection)

At least 16 PBY-3s are undergoing final assembly at the Consolidated plant in San Diego on 8 February 1938. The first two hulls already have markings for VP-9 below the cockpits. The 66 PBY-3s produced were shipped to VP-4, VP-5, VP-9, and VP-16.

This diagram indicates the key difference between the PBY-2 from the PBY-3: the PBY-2 had an updraft carburetor with the air intake below the engine nacelle, while the PBY-3 had a downdraft carburetor with the air intake atop the nacelle between the exhausts.

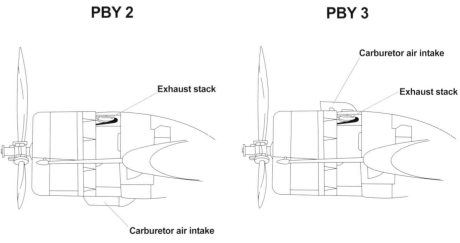

PBY 2

PBY 3

Carburetor air intake

Exhaust stack

Exhaust stack

Carburetor air intake

Consolidated Aircraft and the U.S. Navy inked a contract on 18 December 1937 for 33 PBY-4s. The main substantive change in the PBY-4 from the PBY-3 was the new Pratt & Whitney R-1830-72 engine, rated at 1,050 horsepower, an increase of 150 horsepower over the PBY-3's Pratt & Whitney R-1830-66 engines, rated at 900 horsepower. About the only visually discernable difference between the PBY-4 and its immediate predecessor was the addition of propeller spinners, although a small number of PBY-2s and PBY-3s apparently were briefly retrofitted with spinners. Seen here is a PBY-4 assigned to VP-13. (National Museum of Naval Aviation)

Before World War II, the Marine Corps developed a force called the air infantry: assault troops that were transported and landed by aircraft. Members of a USMC air infantry battalion stand with their equipment with a PBY-4 of VF-12 in the background. (National Archives)

Another group from a USMC air infantry brigade pose for their photograph near the same PBY-4 seen in the preceding photograph. Air infantry troops were distinct from paratroopers in that they rode their aircraft all the way, or close, to their destination. (National Archives)

A member of a USMC air infantry brigade hands an equipment pack to another Marine inside the port waist hatch of a PBY-4 of VP-12 on 25 March 1941. A boarding ladder is attached to the hatch, and the wild goose insignia of VP-12 is on the side of the hull. Formerly designated VP-9, VP-12 would once again be redesignated on 1 August 1941 to VP-24 and assigned to Patrol Wing 2 at NAS Kaneohe. On 1 October 1941 the squadron was reassigned to NAS Ford Island, in the middle of Pearl Harbor. (National Archives)

On 2 May 1941, a contingent of an air infantry brigade is preparing to board five PBYs, including at least one that appears to be a PBY-4. Neutrality stars are visible on several of the PBYs. To the far right is PBY number 12 of VP-12, seen in several preceding photos. (National Archives)

A PBY carrying a team of air infantry has just entered the water and is preparing for takeoff. An aircrewman wearing a flying helmet and a harness is standing up in the port waist hatch. Several men are in the water, removing the main beaching gear. (National Archives)

A gunner mans the .30-caliber machine gun in the starboard waist hatch of an early-model PBY. On the left side of the gun cradle is a box for the .30-caliber ammunition. The stirrup, the mount that could be swiveled down to store the gun so that the weapon could quickly be brought back into firing position if necessary, is visible below the cradle. Aft of the hatch is a stencil for a pull-out snubbing post, used for securing a line to the hull. Stencils indicating the locations for attaching a ladder are below the hatch. (Library of Congress)

A PBY-4 of VP-17 is being prepared for a flight to Sitka, Alaska, in the late fall of 1938. Survival gear has been laid out alongside the flying boat for inspection. Some of the items include life jackets, a VP-17 life ring, bedrolls, thermos bottles, and a cook stove. (National Museum of Naval Aviation)

Several PBYs are on the ramp and in the water at the Naval Torpedo Station, Gould Island Facility, in Narragansett Bay, Rhode Island, in 1939. The plane in the water to the far right has markings for VP-54. The Navy proof-tested its torpedoes at Gould Island. (National Museum of Naval Aviation)

An officer on the ground gives hand signals to the man standing on the starboard engine nacelle of a PBY and straining to hear the officer's orders. This aircraft has the propeller spinners associated with the PBY-4. Numerous fine details are visible on the original print, such as a curved section of rough, non-slip finish on the side of the bow underneath the pendant between the anchor-box door and the front of the chine rail. Where the shadow of the propeller falls on the side of the hull between the national insignia and the numeral 2 is a thin strip of metal that acted as a shield if the propeller should cast off chunks of ice. This feature dated back to the PBY-2. (Stan Piet Collection)

The Transatlantic was a Consolidated Model 28-4, a civilian version of the PBY-4, flown by American Export Lines to investigate potential airline routes from the United States to Europe in 1938. In place of the bow turret, there was a streamlined fairing. (San Diego Air and Space Museum)

The final four PBY-4 aircraft featured improved waist gun positions distinguished by large blisters rather than the sliding hatch. The new style blister was carried forward into subsequent Catalina production. This is the fourth from final PBY-4. (National Museum of Naval Aviation)

PBYs up to the PBY-3 did not have a spinner over the propeller hub. PBY-4s added a spinner to the propeller, offering a useful identification aid for that model of flying boat. However, a few earlier PBYs are known to have been retrofitted with propeller spinners.

Patrol Squadron 18 was one of the units to receive PBY-4s. This example, number 6 of the squadron, is poised on beaching gear on a ramp at a U.S. Coast Guard station in early March 1939. Aluminum paint is on the wing and hull, with black on the hull bottom. (National Archives)

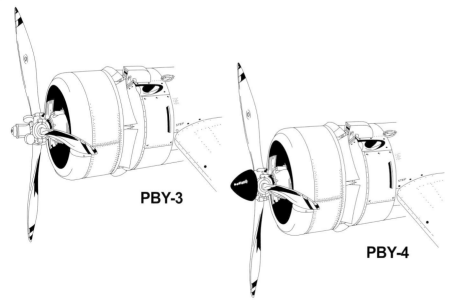

PBY-3

PBY-4

PBY-5 number eight of VP-52 is being towed at NAS Norfolk. The PBY-5 reflected modifications that had been made to the last four PBY-4s, including the substitution of clear blisters on each side of the waist for the sliding hatch doors; redesigned engine cowls, rudder, and vertical fin; and oil coolers moved to the bottoms of the engine nacelles. The horizontal stabilizers and elevators were redesigned and enlarged. In yet another power plant upgrade, Pratt & Whitney R-1830-82 engines were installed. (National Museum of Naval Aviation)

Waist gunner position

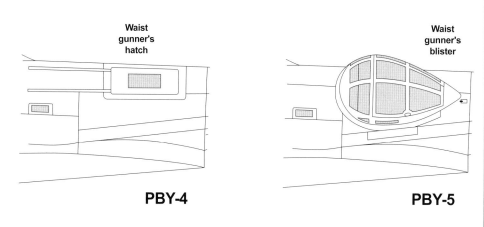

PBY-4   **PBY-5**

With the PBY-5, the sliding hatches in the waist of preceding models of PBY were eliminated in favor of large blisters with Plexiglas windows and metal frames. These blisters provided the waist gunners with a much greater field of vision.

U.S. Navy Ordnanceman Jesse Waller is viewed from another angle with an M1919 .30-caliber machine gun at NAS Corpus Christi, Texas, in August 1942. The box to the gunner's left holds ammunition; the smaller box to his right collects spent casings. (Library of Congress)

The waist blisters of the PBY-5 had a pivoting section in the middle which, when rolled open, allowed the gunner to point his flexible machine gun out into the open. Here, Ordnanceman Jesse Rhodes Waller mans a Browning M1919 .30-caliber machine gun. (Library of Congress)

An M2 .50-caliber machine gun is seen mounted in a PBY-5's starboard waist in August 1941. The frame on which the gun is mounted is called the adapter. Extending up from the side of the adapter is a fitting for a telescopic sight. (National Archives)

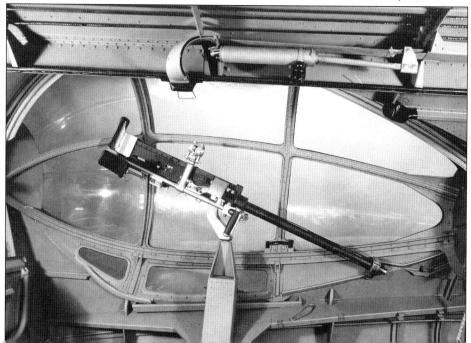

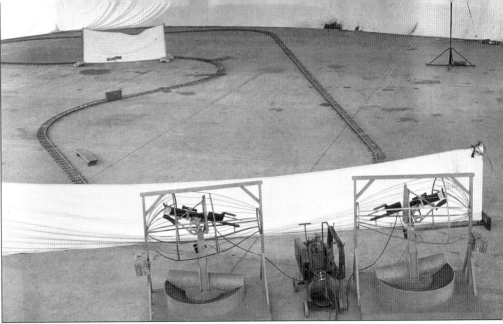

The waist gunners' compartment is viewed facing forward. To the left is a stowed machine gun. The gunners' seats are provided with seat belts. Below the oblong door in the forward bulkhead, which leads to the bunk compartment, is a fire extinguisher. (National Archives)

In the foreground are gunnery practice apparatuses simulating a port and starboard PBY blister gun mount. The air compressor apparently supplied high-pressure air to the practice guns, which would then "shoot down" targets on the track in the background. (Stan Piet Collection)

Natives maneuver a small boat next to the port waist blister of PBY-5 BuNo 2293, the seventh plane of VP-52. It is anchored in the Essequibo River in British Guiana on 12 February 1941. This aircraft was that of the leader of the third section of the squadron. (National Museum of Naval Aviation)

The number six PBY-5 of Patrol Squadron 52 rests on the ramp at NAS Quonset Point, Rhode Island, on 26 March 1941. The hull and the bottom of the wing were painted aluminum, with a thin black band around the hull at the waterline. (National Museum of Naval Aviation)

The nacelles of a PBY-5 are displayed in a January 1941 photo. The cowl flaps are open. Between the nacelles is a radio direction finder (RDF) loop antenna. Within the wing between the engines were integral fuel tanks; two fuel vents protrude from the wing. (National Archives)

These diagrams indicate the redesign of the engine nacelle and exhausts from the PBY-4 to the PBY-5. The carburetor intake was moved from atop the nacelle to the top front of the cowl, and the oil cooler was moved from the wing to below the nacelle.

The port engine nacelle of a PBY-5 is displayed in a December 1940 Consolidated factory photo, providing a good view of the oil-cooler fairing under the nacelle. The blades of the Hamilton Standard propeller are wrapped with protective paper. (National Archives)

A PBY-5 sits on a ramp on 29 April 1941, providing a three-quarters rear view from its port side. A crew access ladder is hanging from the side of the hull adjacent to the port blister. A neutrality star with red circle in the center is visible on the hull adjacent to the cockpit. (National Archives)

Engine development

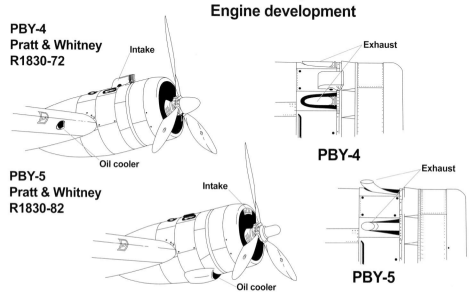

PBY-4
Pratt & Whitney
R1830-72

Intake

Oil cooler

Exhaust

PBY-4

PBY-5
Pratt & Whitney
R1830-82

Intake

Oil cooler

Exhaust

PBY-5

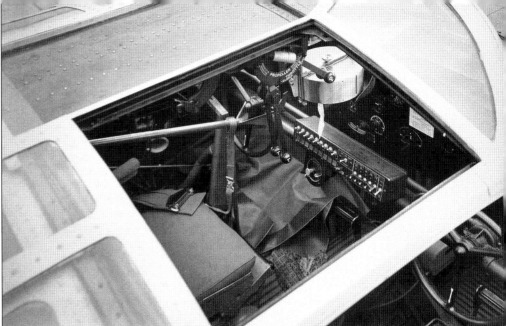

Seen here from the starboard side, this PBY-5 is most likely painted in Nonspecular Blue Gray on the upper surfaces and sides of the hull and the top of the wing, and Nonspecular Light Gray on the undersides of the hull and wing. (National Archives)

An officer and the copilot of a PBY-5 of VP-51 exchange a document. The aircraft has the Nonspecular Blue Gray and Nonspecular Light Gray camouflage scheme and a neutrality star. The RDF loop antenna is barely visible behind the propeller blade. (National Museum of Naval Aviation)

As on preceding models of the PBY, the PBY-5 canopy had sliding hatch doors. Inside the copilot's hatch, a torpedo director is visible below the forward inboard corner of the hatch. Attached to the pilot's control wheel is the aileron and elevator locking bar. (National Archives)

Changes were made in the vertical fin and rudder of the PBY-5, resulting in a straighter trailing edge for the rudder. The RDF loop antenna was moved from the cockpit canopy on the PBY-4 to the top of the center section of the wing on the PBY-5.

Tail Development

DF Loop Development

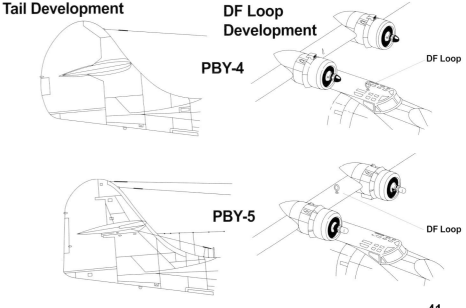

PBY-4

DF Loop

PBY-5

DF Loop

An "eyeball" turret, a late type of PBY bow turret with a bulging Plexiglas window at the front, has been fitted on this PBY-5; the turret is traversed toward the starboard. White bars have been added to the sides of the national insignia, a measure instituted in 1943. (National Museum of Naval Aviation)

This PBY-5 was photographed on the occasion of the first visit of a PBY to the seaplane base at Crescent Harbor, Washington, in December 1942. A close inspection of the photo discloses that under the wing are Yagi radar antennas, bomb racks, and torpedo racks. (Tracy White collection)

Three PBY-5s fly in formation over a shoreline. They have neutrality stars with red circles and are painted in the scheme of Nonspecular Blue Gray on the tops and sides of the hull and the tops of the wing, and Nonspecular Light Gray on the bottom surfaces. (Stan Piet Collection)

PBY-5s assigned to VPB-2 at NAS Jacksonville, Florida, fly in formation on 17 April 1945. Variations are visible in the paint schemes of the three Catalinas; for example, the second and third planes have light-colored pylons, which the first plane lacks. (National Museum of Naval Aviation)

Preparations are underway to beach a PBY-5, unit/aircraft code J1-P-11. The man in the water to the front of the aircraft is giving directions to the pilot for proper positioning. Once the plane shuts down its engines, beaching gear will be installed. (Stan Piet Collection)

In a continuation of the scene in the preceding photograph, the PBY-5 is being prepared for towing, tail first, up the seaplane ramp. Fortunately for the beaching crew, the water is warm, and they can wear swimsuits while attaching the beaching gear and tow lines. (Stan Piet Collection)

Beaching crews were not always as lucky as those in the preceding photo. This crew has donned wetsuits prior to getting into the water to retrieve a PBY-5. Lines are attached to the hull aft of the starboard blister, inside of which several aircrewmen are standing by. (Stan Piet Collection)

The beaching gear has been installed, the swimmers of the beaching crew are clearing the water, and an Oliver tractor is making ready to tow the PBY-5 out of the water and up the ramp. One of the PBY's crewmen is watching the proceedings from atop the wing. (National Museum of Naval Aviation)

A PBY-5 banks over mountainous desert terrain. The clean condition of the paint and the lack of unit markings suggest this is a newly minted plane making a test flight. The tube atop the starboard engine nacelle was a heat exchanger for the wing deicing system. (National Museum of Naval Aviation)

Flying above Mount Katmai, Alaska Territory, in 1941 is a PBY-5 of VP-42. This volcano's eruption in 1912 ranked as the second largest volcanic eruption in the world in the twentieth century. The squadron had been refitted with new PBY-5s in January 1941. (National Museum of Naval Aviation)

A beaching crew tends a PBY-5 while a tractor waits on the ramp. The aircraft appears to be finished in an RAF camouflage scheme with the top of the wing and the fuselage above the waterline are painted Extra Dark Sea Grey and Dark Slate Grey, with Sky below the waterline. (Stan Piet collection)

The British and Commonwealth countries flew various models of the PBY, including PBY-5s designated as Catalina I. Here, a Royal Australian Air Force Catalina I, registration number A24-18, is on a ramp. It was shot down near Bougainville in May 1942. (San Diego Air and Space Museum)

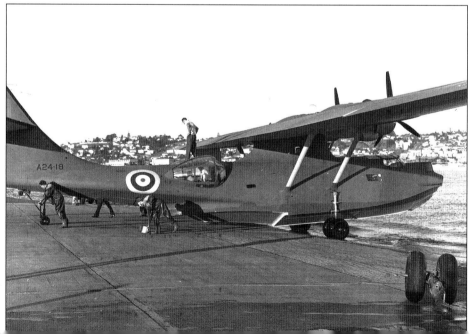

An RAF Catalina I flies over a spit of land. The British began receiving Catalinas in late 1940. A typical camouflage scheme for RAF Catalinas was Extra Dark Sea Grey and Dark Slate Grey, with Sky on the bottom of the hull and the bottom of the wing. (San Diego Air and Space Museum)

Royal Canadian Air Force Canso 9706 appears to have been painted overall in aluminum paint, with a thin black band around the hull at the waterline level. The Royal Canadian Air Force operated PBYs under the name Canso, including this PBY-5, which was delivered on 8 September 1941. (San Diego Air and Space Museum)

As Canso 9706 flies above a shoreline, the pitot tube on the port side of the wing appears to be a British type, with the static sensor offset below the mast. In addition to the U.S. and RCAF, the RAF, the Royal Australian Air Force, and the Royal New Zealand Air Force all flew versions of the PBY. (San Diego Air and Space Museum)

Royal Air Force Catalinas fly on a mission. Catalinas served the RAF well during the Battle of the Atlantic, patrolling the sea lanes, and it was a Catalina crew that discovered the German battleship *Bismarck* when it broke out into the Atlantic in May 1941. (National Museum of Naval Aviation)

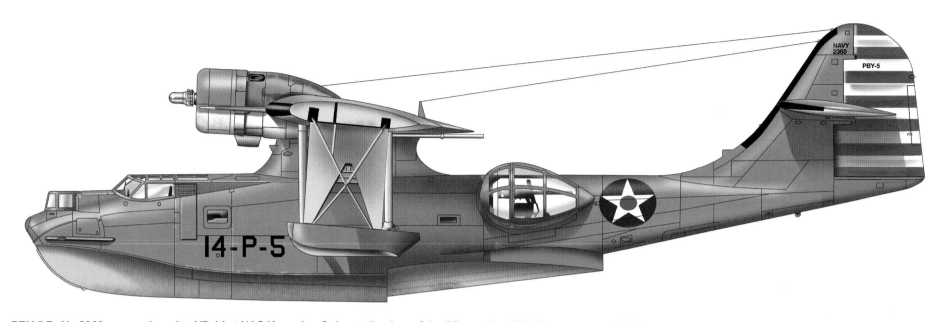

PBY-5 BuNo 2360 was assigned to VP-14 at NAS Kaneohe, Oahu, at the time of the 7 December 1941 Japanese attack. It is shown in the colors and markings it bore from January to May 1942. The basic finish scheme was Blue-Gray over Light Gray.

PBY-5 of VP-23 appears as it did in the Pacific Theater of Operations in 1943. The upper part of the wing and the top and sides of the hull were painted Blue-Gray, and the bottom of the wing and the bottom of the hull were Light Gray. Yagi arrays are below the wings.

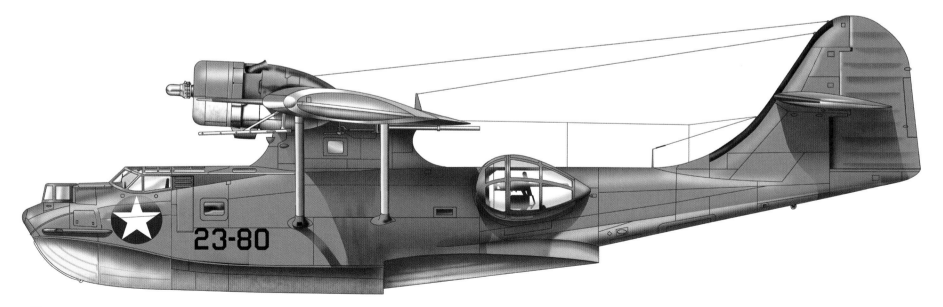

Shown in a 7 December 1939 photo, the final PBY-4, BuNo 1244, was developed into the XPBY-5A, the prototype for the PBY-5A. The XPBY-5A lacked the two waist blisters that were hallmarks of both the PBY-5 and -5A, but included the retractable tricycle landing gear that was a key feature of the PBY-5A. The landing gear could be used for emergency landings on prepared runways or could be used to beach the aircraft. Provisions were still included for mounting detachable beaching gear in situations where the use of that gear was necessary or desired. (National Archives)

47

The XPBY-5A retained the PBY-4's rudder with the curved trailing edge and sliding hatches in the waist compartment. Consolidated Aircraft conducted the initial flight of the XPBY-5A on 22 November 1939 and delivered the plane to the Navy the following month. (National Museum of Naval Aviation)

The port main landing gear is lowered and the beaching gear is attached on the XPBY-5A in a 7 December 1939 photo. Tests showed that the retractable landing gear acted as a sea anchor when the aircraft was on water, making it easier to control during beaching. (National Archives)

A view documenting the XPBY-5, with the main beaching gear on ramps and the bow in the air, provides details of the nose landing gear and doors as well as the retractable metal cover over the bombardier's window. The anchor is hanging by the bow. Above the chine of the hull on each side of the hull is a chine rail, used for securing lines as well as providing a walkway for crewmen when casting out the anchor, securing mooring lines, and performing other tasks. The engine cowls and nacelles retain characteristics of the PBY-4. (National Archives)

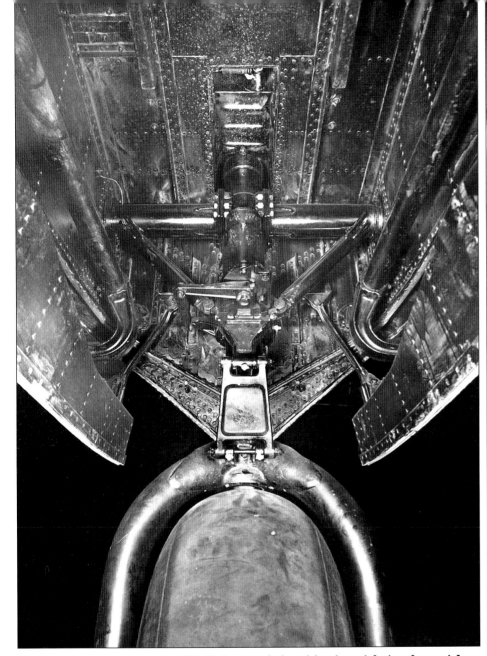

The nose landing gear of a PBY-5A is extended and is viewed facing forward from below the nose landing gear bay. The gear was retracted and lowered by means of a hydraulic cylinder that the pilot controlled, using a selector valve and handle. The gear featured an air-oil shock strut, the torque link of which is visible above the tire. The tire was a smooth-contour type. The landing gear was provided with automatic locks that activated at the end of the retraction process and unlocked at the beginning of the lowering process. (National Archives)

In a 21 October 1941 photograph of the port main landing gear of a PBY-5A, a jack is rigged to the beaching gear fittings to the left. The main landing gear was operated by two hydraulic cylinders: a main cylinder and a smaller one. Above the tire is the top of the oleo strut. The diagonal tube from the top of the oleo strut to the upper interior of the landing gear bay is the main strut. Two V-struts, one over the other, form a linkage from the oleo strut to the lower part of the landing gear bay. A disk cover is over the wheel. (National Archives)

The wheel of the starboard main landing gear of this PBY-5A lacks the cover seen in the preceding photograph. On the oleo strut above the tire is a folding door that covered the top of the landing gear bay when the gear was retracted. Goodrich smooth-contour 47-inch tires were specified for the PBY-5A. The tread of the main landing gear, the distance between the centers of the tires, was 16 feet 9 inches. To the right, on the chine and at the bottom of the wing strut, are fittings for the beaching gear. (National Archives)

The starboard beaching gear is installed on a PBY-5A in a November 1941 photograph. The design was the same as that used on earlier models of the PBY, with long, L-shaped pins securing the strut to a bracket on the chine of the hull, and the top of the strut secured in a fitting in the fairing at the bottom of the forward wing strut. Between the tires is a hand-brake lever. The wheels were Hayes 11.00 x 12 mounting 11.00 x 12 Goodrich smooth-contour, low-pressure tires with Goodrich inner tubes. (National Archives)

The instrument panel in the cockpit of the PBY-5A was fairly spare. The control yoke fitted with control wheels and electrical switch panels, as seen in previous models of the PBY, was still present. Landing gear brake pedals were now atop the rudder pedals. (National Archives)

In a view of the instrument panel and control yoke and wheels of the XPBY-5A, the door in the canvas curtain that provided access to and from the bombardier's compartment is secured shut. The rudder pedals lacked the landing gear brake pedals found on PBY-5As. (National Archives)

With the wheel removed from the starboard main landing gear of a PBY-5A, the complex system of struts and actuating cylinders is visible. At the bottom of the Cleveland Pneumatic Tool Co. oleo strut is the axle. Anti-torque links are positioned at the front and at the rear of the oleo strut. Flexible hydraulic lines are routed from the landing gear bay along the oleo strut and forward anti-torque link. At the center of the landing gear bay is an oval window that allowed inspection of the landing gear from within the plane. (National Archives)

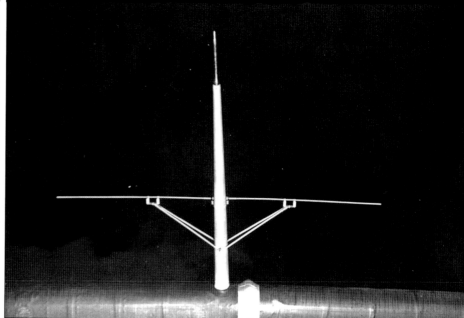

A Consolidated Aircraft factory photo dated 14 November 1941 illustrates an antenna for the ZA blind-landing set that was mounted on the pitot tube on the port side of the wing. Also in view are the deicer boots and the landing light on the leading edge of the wing. (National Archives)

The ZA antenna shown in the preceding photograph is viewed from below, showing the braces that kept the antenna from twisting around during flight. These antennas reportedly have been observed in a number of photographs of PBYs in World War II. (National Archives)

The addition of radar to PBYs greatly extended their ability to search large areas of sky and water. This February 1942 photo shows the Yagi homing transmitting array (left) and the homing receiving array (right) on the bottom of the starboard side of a PBY-5A wing. (National Archives)

On the bottom of the port outer port panel of a PBY-5A wing is a Yagi homing receiver antenna, set at an outward angle from the chord of the wing and supported by two streamlined struts. Also in view is a ZA blind-landing antenna mounted on the pitot tube. (National Archives)

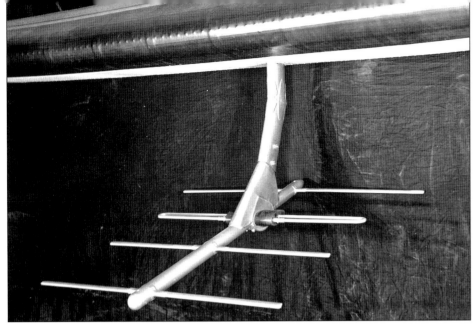

A Yagi transmitting array on the bottom of the starboard panel of a PBY-5A wing is displayed. This antenna sent radar signals which bounced off distant objects; the radar set measured rebounded signals to compute the distance to and bearing of the objects. (National Archives)

The port Yagi homing receiving array is observed close-up, showing the two mounting struts and the support rod with lateral elements. A similar antenna was under the starboard section of the wing, and these antennas received rebounding radar signals. (National Archives)

An installation of Yagi transmitting and broadside receiving arrays on the starboard side of a PBY-5A is documented in an 11 February 1942 photograph. The receiving antenna is the large upper one, and the four smaller ones are transmitting antennas. (National Archives)

This Consolidated factory photo dated 11 February 1942 was intended to document the R.3003 identification friend or foe (IFF) and GO radio antennas, but it also reveals details of a PBY-5A's midsection, including the rear of the breaker step of the hull below the blisters. (National Archives)

On Oahu on 7 December 1941, Japanese forces devastated the PBYs of Patrol Wing 1 at NAS Kaneohe and Patrol Wing 2 at NAS Ford Island. Here, Navy personnel attempt to extinguish flames engulfing a PBY in front of Hangar I at NAS Kaneohe. (National Archives)

Officers and enlisted men heave on a line fastened to a burning PBY at Kaneohe on 7 December. Patrol Wing 1 was equipped with 36 PBY-5s, including three, like this one, moored in the water on that morning. PatWing 1 suffered 27 destroyed PBYs. (National Archives)

In the aftermath of the 7 December attacks, the remains of PBYs are heaped up on a hardstand at NAS Kaneohe. In the foreground is a section of a wing with the float still in the lowered position. Several engines and propellers are in the background. (National Archives)

On the night of 7 December 1941, two Japanese destroyers bombarded Sand Island at Midway Atoll. Several shells struck a hangar, destroying this PBY, the remnants of which subsequently were hauled out of the hangar. Shown here is the bow section. (National Archives)

The waist blisters that became standard with the PBY-5 gave late Catalinas a decided advantage over the earlier models in terms of better field of fire for the waist machine guns and better visibility for the waist gunners, who also served as observers. The blisters had a stationary element, the forward part of which served as a windscreen, as seen on this installation in a PBY-5A. The blisters also had an inner, swiveling section which, when rotated upward, provided an opening for firing the machine gun or for entering and exiting the flying boat. Also in view is a plethora of communications wire antennas. (Stan Piet Collection)

A waist gunner mans a Browning M2 .50-caliber machine gun in the starboard window of a PBY-5A. The .50-caliber machine gun, which boasted better stopping power than the .30-caliber machine guns used in early-model PBYs, was commonly used in blister mounts in the later PBYs. On the right side of the gun is a box for .50-caliber ammunition. On the lower part of the blister are two elongated windows, which gave the gunner the bit of extra visibility that could prove crucial during a patrol mission or a defensive air battle. (Stan Piet Collection)

Attached to the gun mount of this .50-caliber machine gun in a starboard blister is an armor shield. These shields were installed on blister mounts in increasing numbers of Catalinas by the time of the late-production PBY-5s and provided the gunners with a degree of protection from enemy fire. The gun is equipped with a telescopic sight. While these provided a close-up view of the target, they were awkward to use against fast-moving targets. An improvement came when the Mk. 9 illuminated sight was mounted on the blister guns. (Stan Piet Collection)

A close-up of a starboard blister machine gun mount shows the armored shield from the side. The two aluminum-colored tubes to the sides of the pintle mount of the gun are part of the adapter, the shock-buffered frame that the machine gun was mounted on. (Stan Piet Collection)

A 15 May 1942 Consolidated factory photo shows a .50-caliber machine gun in its stored position inside the starboard blister of a PBY-5A. An armored shield is fitted; the stencils on it instructed the installers which way the two plates of the shield were to face. (National Archives)

A starboard blister machine gun installation is viewed facing aft in a 15 May 1942 photograph. Inboard and above the gun is the movable part of the blister, in its raised position. To the left is the aft pivoting mount for the movable section of the blister. (National Archives)

A view of a .50-caliber machine gun in its stored position in a starboard blister shows the bracing and fittings for the armored shield. Mounted on top of a fitting extending from the adapter of the gun is a telescopic sight, to the front of which is the ammunition box. (National Archives)

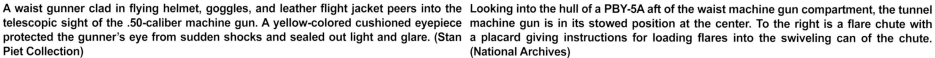

A waist gunner clad in flying helmet, goggles, and leather flight jacket peers into the telescopic sight of the .50-caliber machine gun. A yellow-colored cushioned eyepiece protected the gunner's eye from sudden shocks and sealed out light and glare. (Stan Piet Collection)

Looking into the hull of a PBY-5A aft of the waist machine gun compartment, the tunnel machine gun is in its stowed position at the center. To the right is a flare chute with a placard giving instructions for loading flares into the swiveling can of the chute. (National Archives)

An October 1941 Consolidated Aircraft factory photo shows the tunnel machine gun in its firing position. To the right of the tunnel opening is the stowage bracket for the barrel of the machine gun. Above the gun is the open door for the tunnel opening. (National Archives)

The tunnel gun of a PBY-5A is viewed from the exterior starboard side of the hull. Aft of the ammunition box, the pintle mount of the gun is inserted into the stirrup, the swinging bracket that acts as the gun's support in the firing and the stored positions. (National Archives)

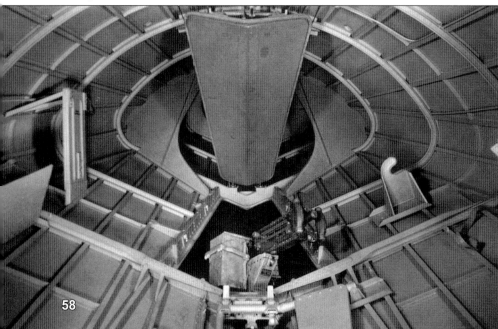

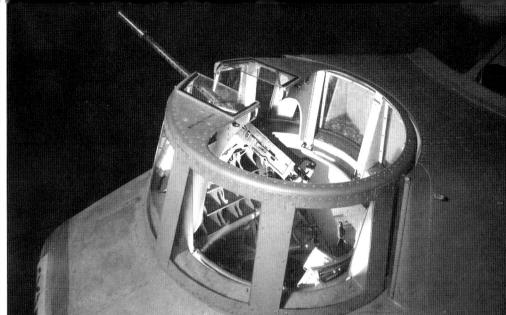

A radio operator makes an adjustment to a RU-19 radio receiver, his other hand poised above a typewriter, at his station aft of the cockpit. He is facing toward the starboard side of the compartment; to the right is the door leading into the mechanic's compartment. (Stan Piet Collection)

The bow turret, as shown on a PBY-5A in a late 1941 photograph, had remained virtually unchanged since the PBY-1. The turret top has been removed, revealing the frame, which was of substantial construction. The .50-caliber machine gun is in firing position. (National Archives)

A small armor plate with a sighting hole cut through it is mounted atop the receiver of the .50-caliber machine gun in a PBY-5A bow turret. Another armor plate is below the ring mount to the front of the receiver. A small window is on each side of the turret roof. (National Archives)

A November 1941 view into a PBY-5A bow turret shows the .30-caliber machine gun in its stored position, seeming proportionally small because of the wide-angle lens used. Below are ammunition racks and the bombardier's kneeling pad and inner window cover. (National Archives)

A gunner grasps the handles of an experimental twin Browning M1919 .30-caliber machine gun mount in a PBY bow turret. The guns are mounted with their ammunition feeds on the outboard sides, and a ring-and-bead sight is attached to the installation. (National Archives)

The same twin Browning M1919 .30-caliber machine gun installation depicted in the preceding photograph is viewed from above and aft. The detachable hard top for the turret is not installed. The ammunition boxes on each side of the mount are visible. (National Archives)

A new bow turret was developed toward the end of PBY production. Called the "eyeball" turret because of the round Plexiglas dome through which twin .30-caliber machine guns protruded, it was introduced starting with PBY-5A BuNo 46580. (National Archives)

A view from another angle of the eyeball turret shows the twin .30-caliber machine guns fully depressed. Another visible feature is the triangular bombardier's window, a feature of late PBY-5As produced at Consolidated's New Orleans plant, and of PBY-6As. (National Archives)

The eyeball turret is viewed from the front. The clear dome flexed with the movement of the machine guns. Contrary to some accounts, the entire turret could be traversed as well. A radome, a late PBY-5A and PBY-6A feature, is visible above the cockpit canopy. (National Archives)

A radome is present over the cockpit of a PBY-5A. Radomes replaced the earlier Yagi radar antennas on late-production PBY-5As and continued to be a feature on the PBY-6A. A protective cover is lashed over the canopy and the eyeball turret. (National Archives)

Crewmen perform routine tasks on a PBY-5A assigned to VP-31. Two men on top of the nacelle of the port engine are engaged in some maintenance chore, while a man on the tarmac is attaching a tow bar to the nose landing gear. The angle of the nose landing gear doors when the landing gear was extended is apparent. The doors began to open before the landing gear began the lowering process, and the doors closed well after the landing gear was retracted. (Stan Piet Collection)

Mechanics work on components in the nacelle of the port engine of a VP-31 Catalina. At least one nacelle panel aft of the open cowl flaps has been removed, and the men are preparing to remove another one. To the rear of the man to the left, on the front of the pylon is a feature introduced with the PBY-5A: a beak-like step built into the front of the pylon, which made it easier for crewmen to climb onto the wing from the deck aft of the cockpit canopy. (Stan Piet Collection)

Another view of the number-eight flying boat of VP-31 shows the mechanics performing maintenance on elements inside the starboard engine nacelle. A Yagi antenna is in view underneath the port side of the wing, and a ZA blind-landing antenna is on the pitot tube. (Stan Piet Collection)

Although PBYs served in Alaska before World War II, after the Japanese invasion of the Aleutian Islands in June 1942, PBYs played a greater role in patrolling the region's vast expanses. Living conditions were basic, as seen in this view of PBY-5s at a base. (National Archives)

PBY aircrews and ground crews in the Aleutians had to contend with horrendous conditions, with mud, snow, and ice frequently being the norm. Here, a crew at Amchitka Island is securing a PBY-5A during a storm. Depth charges are mounted under the wing. (National Archives)

A fuel truck is servicing a PBY-5A in the Aleutians. The hull is severely splattered with mud. Yagi homing receiver arrays are visible below each side of the wing, and four bombs are mounted. The code P-1 is painted in black on the side of the hull. (National Archives)

PBY-5As are assembled at a base in the Aleutian Islands. Catalinas of Patrol Wing 4 were in the front lines of the U.S. defenses against the Japanese invasion. The wing had begun receiving PBY-5As in late January 1942 and radar sets for the aircraft that March. (Stan Piet Collection)

A PBY-5A awaits its next mission at an airfield in the Aleutian Islands on 1 November 1943. On underwing racks are two general-purpose bombs and two depth charges, a typical mix of ordnance, and the bomb cart in the foreground holds another such load. (Naval History and Heritage Command)

A PBY-5A photographed at an Aleutians airfield bears the U.S. national insignia authorized from late June 1943 to mid-September 1943, with a red border around the blue circle and white wings of the insignia. A ladder is attached aft of the blister. (Stan Piet Collection)

Against a backdrop of snowy hills, a PBY-5A of VP-61 conducts a patrol in the Aleutian Islands in March 1943. At that time, the squadron was based at Naval Air Facility (NAF) Otter Point on Umnak Island, with a detachment at NAF Dutch Harbor. (Stan Piet Collection)

The climate of the Aleutian Islands includes extended periods of heavy rainfall and fog, which hampered aviation operations. As a PBY-5A makes a landing on the dirt runway at Amchitka in January 1943, it stirs up a tremendous blast of churning mud. (National Museum of Naval Aviation)

At NAS Dutch Harbor in the Aleutian Islands, a PBY-5A reposes in a revetment created by cutting a gouge into the base of Mount Ballyhoo. As usual for Aleutians-based PBYs, Yagi radar arrays are mounted under the wing, and deicer boots are installed. (Tracy White collection)

As a guard armed with a Thompson submachine gun watches warily to the right, German POWs, survivors of U-164, disembark from a PBY-5A of VP-83 that has delivered them to NAS Natal, Brazil, in February 1943. Depth charges are under each side of the wing. (National Museum of Naval Aviation)

With USS *Wichita* in the background, a PBY-5A is being ferried on the deck of the *Curtiss*-class seaplane tender USS *Albemarle* (AV-5) in a storm off Hvalfjörður, western Iceland, on 15 January 1942. The *Albemarle* measured winds of 82 miles per hour that day. (National Archives)

Two stalwarts of U.S. Navy patrol operations in the Battle of the Atlantic cross paths in 1944: an airship and a PBY-5A of VPB-63. Airships were an important factor in the Navy's antisubmarine operations, patrolling and escorting convoys near the U.S. coast. (National Museum of Naval Aviation)

Crewmen on the bow of a PBY-5A are exiting through the copilot's hatch and the top of the bow turret. Another crewman hunkers down on top of the hull between the waist blisters. As can be seen, the chine rails provided just enough surface for a walkway. (National Museum of Naval Aviation)

A PBY-5A serving with VPB-63 in 1944 displays the Scheme-2 camouflage scheme developed for USN forces engaged in antisubmarine operations in the Atlantic. It comprised Dark Gull Gray on the top surfaces and Insignia White on the rest.

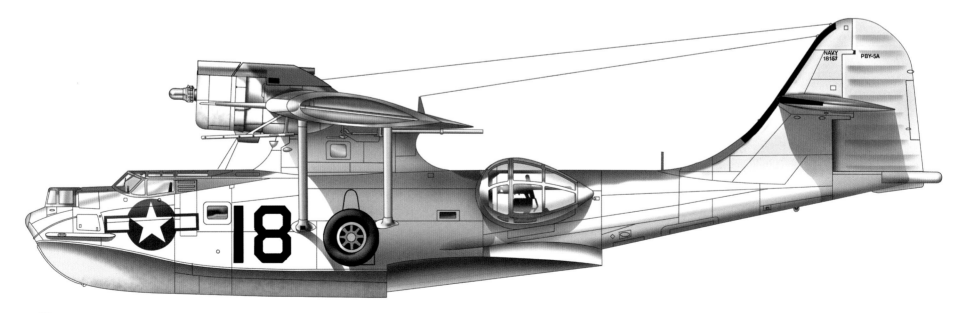

The step protruding from the front of the wing pylon on a PBY-5A is recognizable in this original wartime color photo. Details of the turret and canopy frames, the Hamilton Standard propellers, and the Pratt & Whitney R-1830-92 engines are also visible. (Stan Piet Collection)

A view of crewmen performing maintenance on a PBY-5A with a bomb service truck in the foreground also offers copious details of the bottom of the wing, the starboard landing light in the leading edge of the wing, the wing struts, and the engine nacelles and cowls. (Stan Piet Collection)

A Black Cat PBY-5A is almost touching the water in New Georgia in 1943. The Black Cats were PBY squadrons that specialized in night patrol, artillery-spotting, and attack missions. The first such squadron was VP-12 on Guadalcanal in 1942. (Stan Piet Collection)

Mechanics work on the port blister of a Catalina. The blister hatches were equipped with an inflatable gasket, connected to a hand pump, which sealed off the gap between the swiveling door and the hatch when the door was closed, keeping out drafts and water. (Stan Piet Collection)

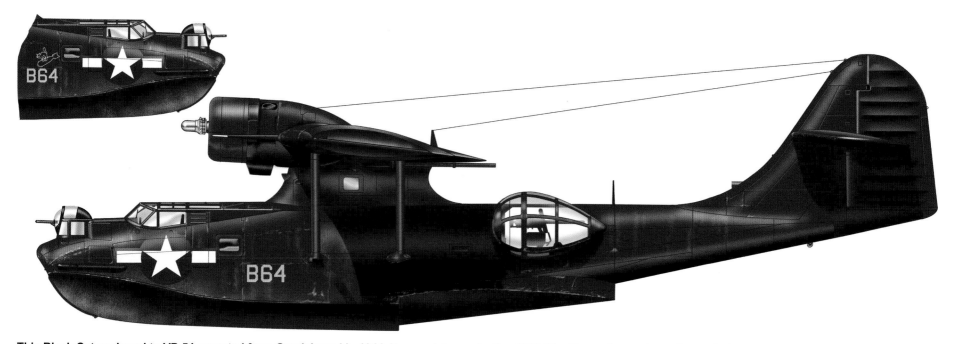

This Black Cat assigned to VP-54 operated from Guadalcanal in 1944. It was a late-production PBY-5A with a radome above the cockpit canopy and an eyeball turret. The code B64 was painted on the hull; the overall paint scheme was matte black.

USAAF OA-10A serial number 44-33879 of the 2nd Emergency Rescue Squadron "Snafu Snatchers" operated in the Southwest Pacific Area. On the hull below the navigator's window was a black scoreboard listing over 50 rescues.

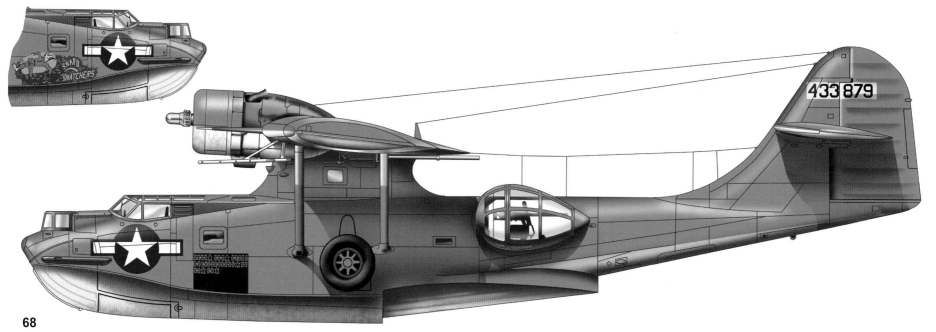

While the U.S. Navy was the prime user of the PBY Catalina, the U.S. Army Air Forces acquired PBY-5As and PBY-6As to use for search-and-rescue aircraft in the vast expanses of the Pacific. Operating in emergency rescues squadrons, these flying boats, given the USAAF designation OA-10s, located and rescued many downed Army Air Forces aircrewmen. Ultimately, the U.S. Army Air Forces received 410 OA-10s of various models. Shown here is OA-10A-VI USAAF serial number 44-33876 of the 2nd Emergency Rescue Squadron "Snafu Snatchers," flying a patrol mission near the Dutch East Indies in 1944. It was one of 230 OA-10A-VIs produced by Canadian Vickers to PBY-5A standards and supplied to the U.S. Army Air Forces. (National Museum of the United States Air Force)

A crowd gathers around OA-10A-VI serial number 44-33879 of the 2nd Emergency Rescue Squadron at Labo, Mindanao, Philippine Islands, in early 1943. Painted below the cockpit is "Snafu Snatchers" and a cartoon of a happy-looking airman on a life raft. (National Museum of the United States Air Force)

OA-10A-VI serial number 44-33879 of the 2nd Emergency Rescue Squadron at Labo, Mindanao, in early 1945 is viewed from the front. Instead of the RDF loop antenna at the top center of the wing, an RDF "football" antenna housing has been installed there. (National Museum of the United States Air Force)

Natives paddle out to a USAAF Consolidated OA-10 anchored in a bay in the Philippines around early 1945. The flying boat had come to land a special reconnaissance party, and Filipinos reported the locations of Japanese naval mines to the crew of the OA-10. (National Archives)

The crew of OA-10A-VI serial number 44-33882 of Flight C, 2nd Emergency Rescue Squadron, pose in front of their Catalina at Middleburg Island, New Guinea, in 1944. The number 82 is on the bow, and auxiliary fuel tanks are mounted under the wing. (National Museum of the United States Air Force)

The OA-10A-VI shown in the preceding photograph, serial number 44-33882, is viewed from the port side at Middleburg Island. Yagi radar arrays are apparent under the wings, and in the upper foreground, a Yagi radar antenna from another aircraft is in view. (National Museum of the United States Air Force)

An OA-10 of the 5th Emergency Rescue Group was photographed in New Guinea. The ubiquitous Yagi radar arrays are present. Previously named the 5276th Rescue Composite Group, this unit was redesignated the 5th Emergency Rescue Group in April 1945. (National Museum of the United States Air Force)

Army OA-10A Catalinas assigned to the Alaskan Division of the Air Transport Command in 1946 wore this colorful scheme of white and insignia red.

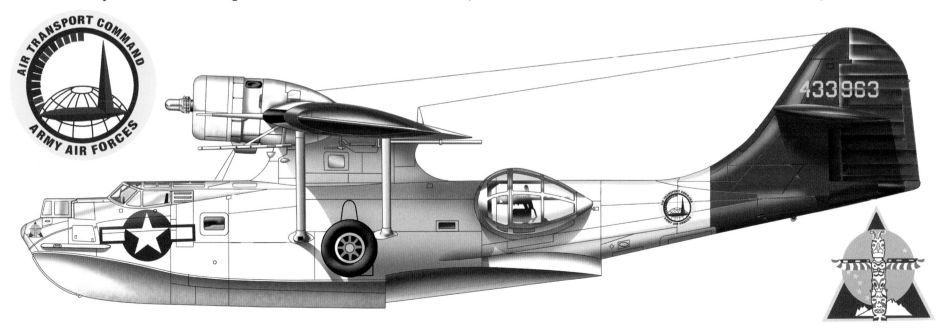

An OA-10 has the self-descriptive name "Air-Sea Rescue" written in attractive script on the side of the hull. Below that name is written in smaller script "Cheryl Ann." In addition to the Yagi radar arrays under the wings, a radome is mounted atop the canopy. (National Museum of the United States Air Force)

Many of the OA-10s featured all-white paint schemes. Black deicer boots are on the leading edges of the wing, horizontal stabilizers, and vertical fin. In addition to the Yagi receiver arrays under the wing, a broadside receiver array is on the hull below the engine. (National Museum of the United States Air Force)

In late 1948, OA-10 44-33950 of the 10th Rescue Squadron prepares for takeoff on a practice mission from Lake Cheletna, Alaska. The aircraft was equipped with two jet-assisted takeoff (JATO) units on each side of the hull below and aft of the blisters. (National Museum of the United States Air Force)

U.S. Air Force OA-10A-VI serial number 44-33939, assigned to the 4th Rescue Squadron at Hamilton Air Force Base, California, sported a very colorful postwar paint scheme, with yellow high-visibility areas and red sections, in addition to the base colors. (National Museum of the United States Air Force)

OA-10A-VI serial number 44-33939 is viewed from the aft port quarter while serving with the 4th Rescue Squadron at Hamilton Air Force Base. On the yellow panel below the cockpit canopy is "ARS4R9" in black letters. Worthy of notice is the manner in which the blue-gray paint wrapped around the bend, or chine, of the hull below and aft of the waist blisters, and also was applied to the vertical part of the step of the hull underneath the waist blisters. Yagi radar arrays are below the wing and a radome is above the cockpit canopy. During World War II, while stationed at Foggia, Italy, this aircraft had an overall white paint scheme. (National Museum of the United States Air Force)

OA-10A-VI serial number 44-33999 boasts a high-visibility scheme for a postwar USAF rescue plane. On the yellow placard below adjacent to the cockpit is "OB-999." The number 999 is in large yellow numerals with black borders on the bottom of the hull. (National Museum of the United States Air Force)

While the 100 Catalina I aircraft had been purchased directly by the RAF, in 1942, Consolidated produced 225 flying boats based on the PBY-5 for delivery to the British via Lend-Lease. Designated the PBY-5B by the U.S. Navy and Catalina IB by the British, serial numbers FP100 to FP324 were assigned to these aircraft. Ultimately, 60 of these were delivered to the U.S. Navy, with 165 going to the RAF. (National Archives)

Intended for delivery to the RAF with serial number FP-216, this PBY-5B was damaged in a water-looping accident in East Bay, Pensacola, Florida, on 28 May 1944, and deemed unfit for furthur flight. It was decided that the hull and a portion of starboard wing would be retained as a training aid, as shown here. This aircraft survives today, as a cutaway exhibit in the National Museum of Naval Aviation. (National Museum of Naval Aviation)

The PB2B-2, a version of the Catalina produced by Boeing of Canada, consisted of a late PBY-5A airframe to which was mated a PBN-1 Nomad empennage. The British and Australians operated them as the Catalina VI and the Americans as the PB2B-2. (National Museum of Naval Aviation)

The PBN-1 Nomad was the U.S. Navy's own take on the PBY Catalina. The Naval Aircraft Factory in Philadelphia, Pennsylvania, developed and manufactured the Nomad, taking the basic Consolidated PBY-5 airframe and redesigning certain elements, including the bow, the bow turret, the floats, and the empennage. The aft part of the fuselage was extended by 56 inches, the fuel tanks were enlarged, and a new bombardier's window was included. Of the 156 PBN-1 Nomads produced from February 1943 to March 1945, the U.S. Navy received 17 and the Soviets received the balance. (National Archives)

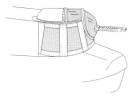

PBY-5A
Twin .30 Caliber guns

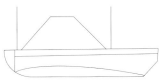

PBY wingtip floats

PBN-1
Retractable power turret
Extended position
one .50 Caliber gun

Bomb window
doors

PBN wingtip floats

The bow turret of the PBN-1 was power operated and had a .50-caliber machine gun. The turret enclosure was convertible, having clamshell sections with clear Plexiglas panels. When raised, these clamshells formed a dome over the lower part of the turret enclosure. (National Archives)

The relative shapes of the eyeball turret of late PBY-5As and the bow turret of the PBN-1 Nomad are illustrated. In the bow of the PBN-1 were doors that covered the bombardier's window. The different designs of the floats of the PBY-5A and PBN-1 are also shown.

With the PBN-1 Nomad's turret clamshell sections lowered and the flat cover removed from the turret enclosure, the receiver of the .50-caliber machine gun, the ammunition box holder, and other elements inside the turret are visible. (National Archives)

When the bow turret of the PBN-1 was not in use, the clamshell sections of the turret enclosure were lowered and a flat cover was placed over the opening at the top of the turret enclosure, both to reduce drag and to give the pilot and copilot better visibility. (National Archives)

The PBY-6A was the final model in the PBY line, produced in 1945 at the Consolidated Aircraft plant in New Orleans, Louisiana. Of 175 built, 52 were delivered to the U.S. Navy, 48 were shipped to the Soviets, and 75 served with the U.S. Army Air Forces as OA-10B-CNs. The PBY-6A shared the late PBY-5A's eyeball turret, tricycle landing gear, and Pratt & Whitney R-1830-92 engines, but added a radome over the cockpit canopy and grafted on the empennage of the PBN-1 Nomad. This USN PBY-6A, BuNo 64063, was part of a 114-plane production block completed between May and September 1945. (National Museum of Naval Aviation)

This PBY-6A was assigned to the Navy Reserve, and as such had orange bands around the aft part of the hull. The paint scheme was Glossy Sea Blue overall; radomes were white. (National Museum of Naval Aviation)

Seen on 11 November 1953 is U.S. Navy PBY-6A, BuNo 64071, based at NAS Barbers Point, Oahu. This PBY later flew under various civilian owners before it crashed and sank in the Tagus River, Portugal, on 28 June 1979. (National Museum of Naval Aviation)

PBY-6A BuNo 46662, photographed on 28 August 1955, was assigned to Corry Field, Pensacola, Florida. The aircraft was painted overall Glossy Sea Blue with yellow hull band and wing panels and splotchy, discolored fabric on the rear half of the wing. (National Museum of Naval Aviation)

U.S. Air Force OA-10B, serial number 45-57834, was assigned to the 1st Rescue Squadron. The aircraft exhibits an overall white paint scheme with a yellow, black-bordered, band near the tail. On the panel adjacent to the cockpit is "AR 1RS." (National Museum of the United States Air Force)

A U.S. Air Force air-sea rescue OA-10A exhibits a postwar paint scheme and markings, including a panel with "OB-939" alongside the cockpit. PBY flying boats performed stellar service in World War II and after. It was PBYs that discovered the German battleship *Bismarck* as it broke out into the North Atlantic, and PBYs that spotted the Japanese fleet as it approached the Midway Islands in June 1942. PBYs helped hold the line in the Aleutian Islands, patrolled vast expanses of ocean, conducted raids, ferried supplies to outposts, and saved many a downed airman. Slow but durable and long-legged, the PBY Catalina was indeed one of the outstanding aircraft of World War II. (Stan Piet Collection)